KENNE>

C000146476

KENNEXSTONE REMEMBERED BY GLYN ROGERS

Compiled by Pat Williams

Published by
The Llanrhidian Local History Group

Copyright © The Llanrhidian Local History Group 2005

Published in 2005 by
The Llanrhidian Local History Group
c/o Big House, Llanrhidian
Swansea, SA3 1ER

A CIP catalogue record for this book is
available from the British Library.

ISBN 0-9547450-1-9

Front cover photograph by kind permission of Chris Elphick

Printed and bound in Wales by
Dinefwr Press Ltd.
Rawlings Road, Llandybie
Carmarthenshire, SA18 3YD

Contents

The Llanrhidian History Group acknowledges the financial support and encouragement of the Gower Society in publishing this book, and the assistance they have received from St. Fagan's Museum of Welsh Life who have provided photographs of the dismantling and reconstruction of Kennexstone Farmhouse. The copyright for these photographs is the property of the National Museums & Galleries of Wales.

Preface

by the Rev. Tudor Lloyd

It is an undeserved privilege to write this preface, but here are some links I have had with the old farmhouse. When, in 1956, many friends asked me where I was going to live as a minister, only two did not ask me where Burry Green was. One was the surgeon, Mr Arnold Aldis, who used to holiday in Llangennith, and the other was a member of our church, Mr Albert Jones. He was a carpenter, and had obtained one of the much sought after posts in the new National Folk Museum, St. Fagan's. He had spent weeks in preparing the old farmhouse for removal to St. Fagan's.

Mr Glyn Rogers' grandmother, Mrs Rogers, then of Kenning House, had seen to it that there was a cooked chicken ready on the vestry table for us on the day I moved into the Manse. When a pipe in the kitchen soon sprang a leak, she ordered Glyn not to leave Mr George Bowen the plumber's side until he came to the rescue. It was Glyn, unprompted, who gave me a regular lift to the Old Walls Guild meetings.

The references to bull-baiting and cock-fighting in Rowland Rogers' farm accounts of 1774 are sad but significant to me. The Methodist Awakening did away with such barbarities, and my own Denomination, the Calvinistic Methodist or Presbyterian Church of Wales, had its beginnings in those days of religious revival.

For all the above links with Kennexstone, and many more, I am glad to write these introductory remarks. Most importantly, however, it enables me to thank Mrs Pat Williams for reviving so much interest in local history. Her energy and industry are phenomenal, and her bright enthusiasm highly infectious. People become eager to answer her questions, and to hunt up information. This has been, and will be, to the enjoyment and enrichment of very many. Mrs Williams deserves our gratitude.

B. Tudor Lloyd

Kennexstone Farmhouse, Llangennith, 1930s.

KENNEXSTONE FARMHOUSE

My family has lived at Kennexstone Farm since the early 17th century. A 'Survay of the Manor of Priorston' taken on the 11th May 1642, names William Rogers gent. as a member of the jury, and mentions 'a place called Kenithstoane.' Priorston was defined as the 'east town of Llangennith'. In the parish records of 1682, John Rogers, Llangennith is named as churchwarden of Llangennith church, and in 1708, John Rogers signed a deed to lease land called 'Rilkethin' from the Rt. Hon. Sir Thomas Mansell. The rent was 20 shillings a year and two capons or 18 pence annually.

'Welch Piety', which was published annually during the 1740s, records that in 1745-46 a circulating school was held at 'Kennickstoane Llangenni', presumably in one of the barns. These were temporary schools that would stay for 3-4 months in one place, usually in the winter months when work was slack. Sixty-seven pupils attended the school.

We had no electricity or water when I was a boy, all the water that we would need for the day's household use would have to be brought from a well one-third of a mile away. We would lead the horses to a nearby pool called the Horse Pool to drink, and there was a stream nearby for the stock. The house was lit by candles and oil lamps. We would cut logs and would always have a huge fire, alongside which was a cupboard bed with sliding doors. This was my bed. It was lovely on a cold night – I could get changed by the fire and next morning get dressed by its warmth. Sometimes, my mother would tuck me up, and then later, when she was cooking supper, she would pass me a sausage through a knothole in the wood. My sister slept upstairs in a small cupboard bed above the charnel, and a servant girl slept in the same room in a four-poster bed. The men servants would sleep above the back kitchen, and my parents above the parlour.

You could look up the chimney and see the sky – my father used to say, "You could drive a horse and cart through it!" When the chimney needed cleaning we would drag a furze bush down it. Flitches and hams hung from hooks in the charnel – a boxlike structure raised above the ceiling – and bunches of herbs would be drying beside them. The farmhouse gun was always hung on a hook alongside the cupboard bed.

Barns at Kennexstone.

A painting of Middle Mill, Burry.
(By kind permission of Mrs. Kathleen Rees, née Harry).

It was always an exciting time when we used the parlour, as we only went into it on special occasions when visitors came to visit, or at Christmas time.

The flagstone floor was washed regularly, but the back kitchen had an earthen floor, which we covered with sand. We brought the sand in a horse and cart from the beach at Llangennith. It would be changed twice a week.

Next to the house was a 3-tie cow stall. We would milk all the cows by hand, and then the milk would be separated – the skimmed milk fed to the pigs, and the cream would be made into butter. Next to the cowshed was the barn. We kept a Lister engine here that would drive our chaff cutter and corn mill. Alongside the barn was a loose box for cattle, and a stable for the horses – over the stable was the granary. We would use our mill to grind barley for the cows, cattle and pigs, and oats for the horses and young calves.

At the far end of the yard was the cart house where we stored the gambos and carts. At the back of the house were the goose nests – six stone nests in a line. When the geese were ready to sit, we would put them onto the nest, each sitting on 6-8 eggs, whilst the gander would stand in front, guarding them from foxes and vermin.

We had an outside bakehouse. My sister would collect dead furze sticks from the common to start off the fire, and then we would add logs. We would light the wood to heat the bake house up, and then later rake over the embers. My mother would bake a week's supply of bread and tarts. Although we had a mill to grind corn for the stock, it was too coarse for bread, so I would take the wheat over to George Harry, Middle Mill, to be ground finely for baking.

My favourite job was going to the forge in Llanmadoc where George Watters was the blacksmith. He could do everything there – re-point harrows, band wheels – whilst I blew the bellows. I still recall the smells and sounds of the old forge, and the conversations that went on there. I remember George asking one old boy:

"Where hast thy been, boy?"

"I've had Louisiana flu," he replied, "but after 14 pints in the Britannia, I drowned her!"

The farming year at Kennexstone

WINTER

I would spend many winter days laying hedges and banking. My son tells me I have laid over seven miles of hedges around our fields. We would repair the hedges with clots, and sometimes we would build new

11

The Forge, Llanmadoc.
(By kind permission of Mrs. M. Harwood, Britannia Inn, Llanmadoc).

ones – building up a bank with clots of earth and planting cuttings of blackthorn on it. We would also cut logs for the house and bakehouse.

We would have the stock to feed, and would clean out the sheds and groom the horses. We were using the horses for ploughing, and farming was very labour-intensive in those days. My father would go to the hiring fair in Brecon to hire men to work on the farm. Many of them stayed in Gower, and married local women. We had two sets of brothers at different times – Elwyn and John James, and Wilfred and Cuthbert Pugh all came to work at Kennexstone. Feeding the stock would take a good part of our time, as they had to be fed four times a day. The hay would be cut with a large hay knife, grain would be ground in our mill, and a pulper used to pulp swedes

From left – Evan Jones, Wilfred Pugh, John Jones, John Rogers and John Prosser.

into chips. We would also feed straw and hay into the chaff cutter and it would come out in small, easily digestible pieces.

We also kept pigs – when we had a litter, we would keep two to provide our bacon for the year. Gordon Rees, Llangennith, was our butcher, and he would come to slaughter the pigs, then they would be salted and cured. The flitches and hams would be hung on hooks in the charnel until needed. We would eat fat bacon for many of our meals, except for Sunday when a joint of beef or lamb was bought.

Our lambs were born early at Christmas-time, so that we would always have lamb for Easter Sunday dinner. The womenfolk would care for the poultry. We kept a few turkeys, but mostly ducks, geese and chickens. Christmas was a very busy time when they had to dress the poultry ready for sale. The feathers would be saved for quilts, and goose wings would be used for dusting. There were also the cows to be milked, and butter to be churned.

*Left, kneeling – Jack Phillips, rabbit catcher, with
Ronnie Gibson, Gamekeeper, Penrice Estate, 1930s.*
(By kind permission of Peter Gibson).

We used to have a great problem with rabbits. There were so many in our fields that we had to fence around them to prevent them getting to the corn. We would spend one day a week ferreting. My neighbour, Ambrose Holland, who worked at Tyle House, would come over with his ferrets and we would catch the rabbits in nets when the ferrets drove them out of their burrows. Strangely enough, we could never do this if the wind was coming from the east – the rabbits would never bolt in an east wind – so the ferrets would go down the burrows and eat the rabbits there. We would have to send another ferret with a line on it to find the first ferret and dig it out. We would also go out on a dark windy night (when the rabbits wouldn't hear you approach) – spread out a net and sometimes would catch as many as thirty in the net. We would sell the rabbits to the butcher; they preferred rabbits with no shot in them. We also had a lot of hares in the fields – you could always tell if they were there, because they would eat a neat circle of corn, unlike the rabbits who ate everything!

We spent a lot of time in winter clearing out the ditches to keep the fields dry. This was all done manually. We would spread dung during the winter months – there was little artificial fertiliser then. I remember Hubert Gordon, Tyle House talking to a man selling artificial fertiliser. The man told him that he only needed a small amount of fertiliser for each field – enough to go into your waistcoat pocket, he was told.

"Aye," replied Hubert, "And you'll be able to take the crop away in the other pocket!"

My father told me that in the days before there were hauliers, when there were cattle to be slaughtered, the men would get together and drive them on foot to the slaughterhouse in Dyfatty. The men would stop at Fairwood Common for the animals to graze, drink in the pool there, and have a rest. They would then go down Walter Road into Swansea, and once, one of the cattle caught sight of his reflection in a shop window, and charged at it breaking the window.

SPRING AND SUMMER

We would start ploughing in March. The horses would be groomed and fed, and then we had our breakfast whilst the horses were having theirs. Great pride was taken in caring for the horses, they got to know and understand you, and without this bond you couldn't expect a good day's work from them. We would have already spread dung on the fields, and after harnessing them we would take the horses out to plough the soil. When ploughing, it is important to get a straight furrow, so we would make a mark on a hedge, line up the horses between the mark, and then run straight for the line. Later we would roller and harrow it to produce a good tilth. We would also open up the rows and plant potatoes, swedes, cabbages and mangolds. We would have help to do the planting, and would give the helpers their individual rows so

Dai Jones Cillibion competing in a West Gower Ploughing Match, 1936.
(By kind permission of Mrs. M. Davies, Knelston).

that they could grow their own vegetables. Later, we would single out the plants with a hoe. We would hire boys from Brecon and Hereford as farm labourers (the Hereford boys would go to the hiring fair in Brecon, looking for work), and on a Sunday, a day of rest when only the stock would be fed, they would go around the different farms to compare the jobs that were being done there. They all took a great pride in their work.

It was always in the springtime that we limed the farmhouse, buildings and walls.

In summertime, we would roll the hay fields to firm the grass down ready to be cut, then clear the field of stones so that the mower would not be damaged. The hay would be cut into swards with the mower, and shaken with a shaker. It was then left until dry. We would rake the hay into rows, and then would attach a sweeper to the horse, and sweep the hay into the ricks.

It was also in the summertime that we washed our sheep. We would block the stream, and put a pen in a field to hold the sheep, and then drive them through the wash. They would later be sheared with a hand-turned shearing machine.

The wool would be packed into sacks, and, as there was no Wool Board in those days, different buyers would come around the farms, and we would take the best price offered. Our sheep were Lowland sheep, and their fleeces were more valuable. They also had to be dipped to prevent flies. We would drive them down to the Burry River – the dip

Hand-turned sheep shears.
(By kind permission of John Doherty).

was at the side of the river – all the farmers working together as a team. Our local policeman, Sergeant Austin, used to stand by the dip, ensuring with a stopwatch that the animals were under the water for the correct length of time.

AUTUMN

This was a busy time, with the harvest to get in. My grandfather would have cut the corn with a scythe – a group of men working in a line across the field. But the reaper and binder had come into use when my father was harvesting. We would build hayricks in the fields, and corn ricks – or 'mows' as we call them in Gower – in the rickyard. We would 'stook' the corn in the fields, 6-8 sheaves in each stook – until it was ready to be stored in the ricks. The grain would be brought into the farmyard in a gambo and the men would begin to build the mow. Beforehand we would have cut bracken, which we would use as a base to keep the grain off the ground. The rick would be built up into a large square, starting in the centre, and then as it grew it would be shaped until only one sheaf was needed to finish the top. The ricks would be thatched with gloy (wheat straw) from the

Reaper and binder, Kennexstone. From left – John Prosser, John Rogers on binder and Emlyn Hughes, Burry Green.

previous harvest, to prevent the corn getting wet. We also would store our potatoes in trenches, and thatch over them, keeping them dry throughout the winter until they were needed.

Thrashing at South Hardings Down Farm. Far left – George Nicholas and behind the steam engine is Cyril Nicholas.
(By kind permission of Susan and Philip Nicholas).

The corn would have to be thrashed – in my grandfather's day men using flails would have done this, but when I was young a thrashing machine would come to the farms. These machines were too expensive for the individual farmer, so they would employ contractors to visit each farm. Llewellyn Gordon, Llanrhidian, owned the engine that used to come to Kennexstone. There would be two thrashing days on our farm, one in spring and the other in the autumn. We would take a barrel down to the Burry River on a horse and cart to fetch water for the engine. Sam Winch and Christie Tucker were the drivers, and they would light up the boiler. When they had 'steam up' they would blow their whistle to let the neighbouring farmers know that their help was needed. About 15 men would help – some feeding the thrasher, but the hardest job fell to the men who had to carry sacks of grain up to the granary.

This was a busy time for the women of the farm who had to provide all the workers with refreshments throughout the day, and then finally a large supper. If it began to rain after the engine arrived, it might be a day or two before the work could be carried out – but the men still needed to be fed! It was a busy time for my dog Bonzo too! He knew that there would be plenty of rats hiding at the bottom of the rick and one year killed 78! One rat ran up my trouser leg, but fortunately I managed to get hold of its head before it could bite me. Bonzo was

Thrashing day, South Hardings Down Farm.
(By kind permission of Susan and Philip Nicholas).

waiting when I got him out – but after that we all made sure that we tied the bottom of our trouser legs.

After the days of the steam engines, the thrashers were driven by tractors. I remember the Field Marshall tractor that would be started by placing a cartridge in a compartment in the engine; this would then be tapped with a hammer. With a loud burring noise it was away!

The thrashing machine had a trusser behind it, which would truss the wheat straw into bundles ready for the next year's rick thatching.

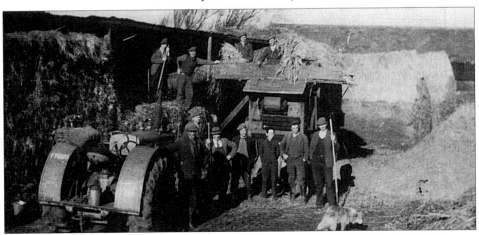

Thrashing in Gower, 1952. Tractor-driven thrashing machine.
Stanley Jones, Cillibion Sawmills, owned this Minneapolis Moline tractor,
which was painted yellow. Alan Gwynn, Llanrhidian, is standing alongside the tractor.
(By kind permission of Donald Lewis).

A sound archivist at the Museum of Welsh Life, St. Fagan's, recorded my mother, Mrs. Gladys Rogers, talking about her life in the old farmhouse in the 1930s. These are her memories.

Gladys and John Rogers.

THE BACK KITCHEN

In our back kitchen was a large cast iron boiler with a lid. We would always need lots of hot water, especially on a Monday which was our washing day, so the boiler was kept going all day. Hot water was also needed for washing the milk churns and butter workers. I had an old-fashioned wooden washing machine – it was similar to a butter churn, with a cover and a handle to turn it. It had a mangle on top. A settle was alongside the wall.

A washerwoman would come to the house on Mondays to help me, as there was always a lot of washing to do. There would be about 10 people living in the house, including family, workmen and maids.

After washing, we would rinse the clothes in a zinc bath, put them through the mangle, and then they would be hung out to dry in the garden. They were later placed around the fire to air overnight.

We kept a small zinc bath in which the workmen would soak their feet after a long day's ploughing. We had a bungalow bath for bath nights – which we kept hanging on a hook in the dairy. Everyone had his or her own bath night!

The back kitchen had an earthen floor, which we would cover with sand. When the workmen came in from the fields in their muddy boots, the sand made it easier to brush away the dirt.

THE KITCHEN

The cooking was done in the kitchen on a black range with an oven, which was alongside the fire. I would cook the meat in the oven, and would place a brandis – an iron stand with four legs – over the fire to hold the bakestone. Every day we would whitewash the side of the fireplace and under the fender, and the grate would be black-leaded. On the mantelpiece was a coffee mill and a little old cupboard in which I used to store spices and nutmeg. The cupboard had SP carved on the front. (Probably belonging to Sarah Roger who married Richard Punner in 1767.)

There was a roasting jack hanging from a beam above the fireplace – I would often use this to cook the meat. I used to wind it up and the meat would turn slowly above the fire.

We would eat in the kitchen – the maid and workmen at one long scrubbed table and the family at a round table by the dresser.

THE DAIRY

The dairy was a large room where the milk-separating and churning took place. We always did the churning on Wednesdays. We kept a cheese press in the dairy, although I didn't make a lot of cheese as it used up all the cream. I needed the cream to make and store enough salt butter for the winter.

There was also a wooden salting tub, which we used when we had killed a pig. We would kill a pig in December and another in January before the weather became too warm. After the butcher had cut the pig up, we would take the sides and hams to the dairy where they would be placed in the tub and covered in salt and saltpetre. The meat would stay in the salting tub for three weeks. The men would then carry it out to the river. They placed a sink alongside the river, and it would be washed. The flitches would later be hung from the charnel until dry. After about six weeks the flitches would be stored side-by-side in a wooden box – each flitch covered in straw. We would also make faggots, and from the feet and head of the pig we would make brawn. My mother-in-law used to make black pudding out of the blood. She would also wash and scrape the intestines and make sausages.

At certain times we would kill our own sheep and lambs. This depended on the work that was going to be done on the farm. If we needed a lot of men to help, like at thrashing or harvest time, we would kill some lambs. We always had fresh meat for thrashing day. We would feed at least 15-16 men, they would be with us for a day and a half usually, but if the weather was bad they would be there longer – and would still need to be fed. Usually we only had fresh meat on a Sunday. Our local butcher in Llangennith killed once a week, and that was our only chance to buy it. He would kill on a Thursday and I would go there on a Friday. I would usually buy beef, which I would roast, and it would last a few days.

We kept all our food in the dairy. It was stored in a food safe with an openwork front.

THE PARLOUR
The parlour was our best room, which we used when we had visitors. There was a large sampler on the wall, that had been embroidered by my husband's grandmother.

This sampler was made by Mary Hoskins in 1852.

THE BEDROOMS

The menservants could only reach their bedroom by going through the maid's room. This meant that they had to go to bed before the maid, so that they would not disturb her. We had another staircase built that led directly to their room. The bedrooms were simply furnished with a bed and washstand. The floor was covered in oilcloth and rugs.

The thatch was covered inside with a type of hessian or canvas, and was whitened over with a lime wash. The bedrooms were cold and draughty. If you took a candle upstairs it would be blown out!

Under the stairs was a cupboard that we called the wine cellar. Here I stored jams, elderberry wine and mead.

On Tuesdays I did the ironing, using a box iron, although my mother-in-law used to use a flat iron that had to be heated in front of the fire. The clean blankets and sheets would be stored in coffers alongside the cupboard bed.

On Fridays we would bake the bread and tarts. The outdoor bakehouse had to be lit two hours before the baking began. The bread would rise whilst the bakehouse reached the correct temperature. We always knew when it was ready, as the bricks would turn white with the heat. We had a special rake with a hook on one end, to remove the tins when the bread was cooked. I would bake eight loaves of bread –weighing 6lb each – and three fruit tarts. I would put tarts into the oven at the same time as the bread, and after twenty minutes they would be removed. I would then put in a slab cake that would be ready at the same time as the bread.

We used our own flour for bread making. It would be brought back from Middle Mill in sacks, and then stored in a flour bin. The bread was stored in a large wooden box that I kept in the dairy.

Saturdays were spent cleaning and polishing. I would make my own beeswax polish, as we kept our own hives. The honeycombs would be melted in boiling water, and then strained into a bucket. The wax would be skimmed off, melted and mixed with turpentine, until it became a paste. It was then stored in small pots. We would use the paste to polish all our furniture; no woodworm would touch it then!

We had three hives at Kennexstone. The honey had a beautiful flavour as the hillside nearby was covered in heather. We would all help to extract the honey – we had a machine that would spin the combs. The honey was then bottled immediately and some was sold to local customers – though we kept a good supply for the farmhouse.

Mead was usually made in the autumn in readiness for Christmas. After the honey had been extracted, the combs would be soaked in a huge pan of cold water for a day or two. The water would then be boiled and strained, and sugar and ginger would be added. This would then be stored in stone jars in our wine cellar.

To cure our coughs and colds, we would mix honey, vinegar, butter and lemon, and then stand it in a saucepan of hot water until it dissolved. We had wonderful faith in that!

We had a kitchen garden with vegetables – peas, beans, carrots, parsnips and beetroot. Potatoes, cabbages and swedes were grown in the fields. There were gooseberry and blackcurrant bushes and a pear tree close to the house and we also had a large apple orchard. A tall monkey-puzzle tree was in front of the house, and in the front garden we grew flowers.

Every year the thatch would need some repairs – but only on the outside. Storms and birds did the most damage. The straw would be brought from Devonshire – it was much better at keeping out the rain than our local straw.

As there was no bus from Rhossilli to Swansea in those days, the fishermen would have to sell their catch locally. They would come around the Gower villages in their gambos selling fresh bass or flat fish. We were always glad to have fresh fish. The village boys would put out herring nets and would collect them twice a day, and if they had a good catch, we would buy them and salt them down. We would put the herrings into earthenware pans – with a layer of salt on the bottom. They would then be covered with a sprinkle of salt. They would remain in the pans until we needed them. I would have to soak them before cooking. We would usually toast them in front of the fire on a toasting fork. An old woman would also walk to our farm from Rhossilli carrying a basket on her head containing laverbread and crabs. I would cover the laverbread in oatmeal and cook little cakes of it in bacon fat for breakfast.

Women would visit us from Penclawdd as well. They would walk around Gower carrying cockles – one basket of cockles on their heads and another on their arms. The ones on their arms were the cockles still in the shells, and were much heavier. The cockle women would be dressed in Welsh flannel. I would boil the cockles in the shell for tea with bread and butter. Those out of the shell I would fry with leeks, and we would have them for breakfast.

I would send our surplus eggs to a grocer in Swansea by bus. I would include my shopping list – usually tea, sugar, currants, dried fruit and oatmeal – the grocer would collect the eggs from the bus, take out the money that I owed him, and then would send the groceries back on the bus with my change.

At sheep shearing time, we would always take some of our wool to the Factory in Llanmadoc to be made into quilts, blankets and suits. The weaver there was Billy Tanner.

At hay harvest or sowing time, I would send meals out to the fields for the farm workers. The meat would be put into a milk tin, (a large tin that was used to separate the buttermilk and cream in the days before mechanical separators) and surrounded by vegetables. A jug of gravy was placed in the centre and the plates were put over the top. This would be tied up tightly in a thick cloth and taken to the fields.

At breakfast time – about 8 o'clock, after milking – I would make porridge and boiled or fried bacon and eggs. We all ate together – family and farm workers. The maid would help me prepare the food, but I did all the cooking. I would sometimes make broth in the wintertime. I would buy bones from the butcher, boil them up for a few hours and then in the morning add leeks and parsley. This would be served with bread.

Dinnertime was at 1 o'clock. I would prepare boiled bacon or rabbit – as we had plenty of those about! I would cook them in different ways – perhaps baked or stewed. We would sometimes kill a fowl and have it boiled or roasted. There was always a pudding – boiled, steamed or rice.

Our teatime was at five o'clock. We would have bread and butter, jam, cheese and cake.

Suppertime was between 9 and 10 o'clock. Sometimes we had sausages, or boiled bacon.

My Recipe Book

Whitepot

I would make whitepot for a light summer supper, or it could be carried out hot to the fields as a pudding for the farm workers during the hay harvest. It was easy to carry as it was made in one big pan. I mixed flour, milk and sugar – though some people used boiled rice instead of flour. It was then baked and served hot with cake or bread and butter.

Dowsett

I remember my mother-in-law telling me that when the baking was done on a Friday, they would put in a big tin of dowsett in the oven, so that when they were cleaning on a Saturday, they didn't have to stop to prepare a meal. To make dowsett, I would line a pie dish with pastry, and mix together eggs, flour, milk, salt, sugar and spice. When it was cooked it resembled custard tart.

Pease pudding

Pease pudding was served with salted beef or pork. The peas were soaked in cold water overnight, then wrapped in a cloth and put in a saucepan of salted water. The peas were boiled for 2-2½ hours, then strained and pressed through a sieve. Butter, a beaten egg, salt and pepper were added and a little bit of sugar. The mixture was tied up in a floured cloth and boiled again for 30 minutes. It was then served with the meat.

Parsley pie

We often had parsley pie for tea – it would be eaten cold. We ate it all year round. This again was a pie dish lined with pastry; beaten eggs would be added, flavoured with parsley and sugar. It was thickened with a little flour and baked.

Cheese cakes

I made these when I could spare the milk – it took a good drop of milk to make them. I would heat the milk to blood heat, put rennet into it and let it curdle. I would drain the curds and hang them in a cloth to dry. I would then mix currants, sugar and spice into the curds, roll out my pastry and put the curds into a rounding. I would fill half of it, and then turn the pastry back over and bake them on a bakestone. These were for afternoon tea or to be sent to the field.

We also needed to keep the men well supplied with drinks at harvest time.

Haytime Nectar

To make Haytime Nectar, we would boil a gallon of water with 2lb of sugar, 3 lemons and 1lb of raisins. The water was allowed to cool, then stirred daily for three or four days to allow it to ferment. It would turn colour – it would resemble lemonade – then it would be strained through fine muslin into bottles. It was diluted before drinking.

Nettle pop

I would take a handful of dandelion leaves, a handful of nettle leaves, a handful of ground ivy and a stick of rhubarb – blackcurrant leaves were very good in it too! I would cover the leaves with water, and boil them for about ten minutes in a large saucepan, then strain the liquid and add a pound and a half of sugar and ½oz of yeast. The following day we would strain the liquid again and put it into earthenware jars. We would take a lot of this out to the fields where it would be served undiluted.

Glyn Rogers

In 1939, my parents moved into our new house Bryn View, which had been built on our land, and the old farmhouse was then used for storage, although as we had no local thatchers since Phil Bowen of Rattle Street, Llanmadoc, had died, it was difficult to keep it in good repair.

One day in 1950, as my father and I were working in the yard, a man approached us and introduced himself as Dr. Iorwerth Peate, the Director of the museum at St. Fagan's. In 1946, the Earl of Plymouth had offered St. Fagan's Castle, with its gardens and grounds to the National Museum of Wales. It was Dr. Peate's intention to establish a folk museum on the site, similar to ones he had seen in Scandinavia. He wanted to have one building from all the old counties of Wales, and he had chosen Kennexstone to represent Glamorganshire. He asked my father if he would allow our farmhouse to be rebuilt in St. Fagan's. We agreed, and plans were put in motion to dismantle and transfer the building.

In 1950, a team of surveyors and builders arrived in Gower and stayed for many weeks at the King's Head Hotel in Llangennith until the work was completed. They measured the farmhouse, and marked every stone and piece of timber with a number.

The old farmhouse was eventually moved in 1951 by Wynn's Transport, Newport. It took 38 lorry loads, and even the cupboard bed I had

Kennexstone Farmhouse, at Llangennith, 1950.

The scissors roof truss, and woven straw matting.

slept in as a boy was taken. During the dismantling process, the men discovered an old wooden slatted window from an age before glass was used, and behind the modern grate they found another that still did not match the date of the house. The wall was six foot thick, so they dug back a little further, and found the original oven. Kennexstone Farmhouse was amongst the first buildings to be transferred to St. Fagan's.

The goose nest beside the back door.

In 1777, Marrish Richard was paid 6d for 'making a goose house'.

Reconstruction at St. Fagan's, 1952. Dr. Peate can be seen on the far right.

Kennexstone Farmhouse at the Welsh Folk Museum

The cost of re-erecting the farmhouse in St. Fagan's was assisted by a grant from the Welsh Committee of the Festival of Britain in 1951. Museum research dates the house to about 1630, when only the eastern end of the present building would have existed. The kitchen area was added later, and the complete house renovated in the 18th century, when the back kitchen and windows were added. In the kitchen was a recess in the ceiling, known as a charnel, which was used for hanging bacon. The original cupboard bed and kitchen benches were also taken to the museum.

Thatching at St. Fagan's. The straw mats can be seen under the thatch.

The roof is thatched, and intricately woven straw mats form the under-thatch. The museum had great difficulty in finding a thatcher with the expertise to do this, but eventually tracked Mr. Davies down in Cardigan. These mats, extending from the ridge to the eaves, rest on the purlins,

D. J. Davies making the under-thatch for Kennexstone.

29

Final stages of rebuilding.

Kennexstone at St. Fagan's.

and make rafters unnecessary. They are bound to the purlins by bramble strips.

In St. Fagan's, the house has been furnished in the style of 1790, and as was customary then, the farmhouse has been painted red to protect it and its occupants against evil spirits, and a red-berried rowan tree was planted in the garden for the same purpose.

I have visited St. Fagan's museum many times with school trips. Here I am with the children of Bishopston School alongside my cupboard bed, telling them what it had been like to live in the old farmhouse.

At present, plans are underway to move the barns that were adjoining the old farmhouse to St. Fagan's, so the farmhouse and barns will finally be reunited.

Burry Green visits St. Fagan's

In August 2003, Burry Green chapel organised a Sunday School excursion to the Museum of Welsh Life at St. Fagan's. Seventy local people turned up for the trip, and we spent a wonderful day at the museum. My sister Vera and I were able to give the group a conducted tour of the old farmhouse.

MY FAMILY

The Rogers family, 1960.
Back row – Cecil Thomas, Ivy, Vera Thomas (née Rogers), and Glyn.
Alan, John Rogers (holding David), Gladys Rogers (holding Ian), Christopher.

In a terrier or land inventory for the parish of Llangennith dated 1720, John Rogers and Richard and Thomas France are amongst the parishioners of Llangennith who signed the document.

The two families were later united by the marriage of Rowland Rogers, Kennexstone, and Mary France on the 3rd January 1752/3.

The terrier records the tithes due to the vicarage of Llangennith, in 1720:

> *Item.* There is due at the feast of Easter, yearly for offerings from every married couple Three pence, from every widdower or widdow one penny half penny, from every single person above the

33

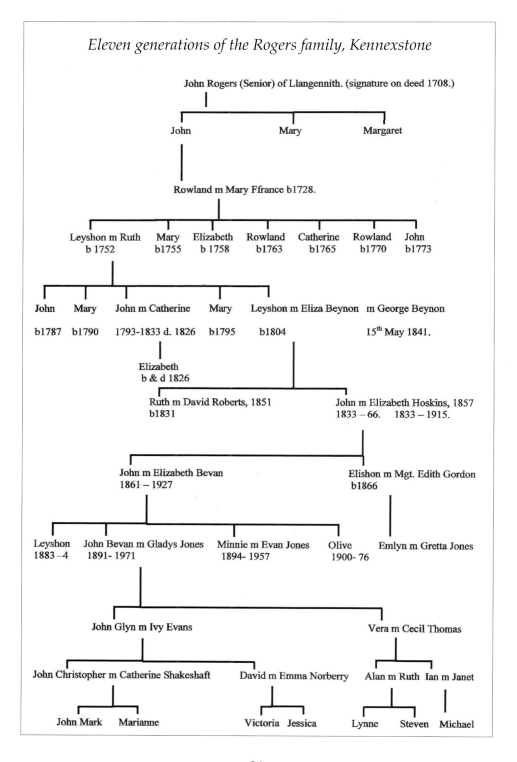

Eleven generations of the Rogers family, Kennexstone

John Rogers (Senior) of Llangennith. (signature on deed 1708.)

John   Mary   Margaret

Rowland m Mary Ffrance b1728.

| Leyshon m Ruth b 1752 | Mary b1755 | Elizabeth b 1758 | Rowland b1763 | Catherine b1765 | Rowland b1770 | John b1773 |

| John b1787 | Mary b1790 | John m Catherine 1793-1833 d. 1826 | Mary b1795 | Leyshon m Eliza Beynon b1804   m George Beynon 15th May 1841. |

Elizabeth b & d 1826

Ruth m David Roberts, 1851 b1831   John m Elizabeth Hoskins, 1857 1833 – 66.   1833 – 1915.

John m Elizabeth Bevan 1861 – 1927   Elishon m Mgt. Edith Gordon b1866

| Leyshon 1883 –4 | John Bevan m Gladys Jones 1891- 1971 | Minnie m Evan Jones 1894- 1957 | Olive 1900- 76 | Emlyn m Gretta Jones |

John Glyn m Ivy Evans   Vera m Cecil Thomas

John Christopher m Catherine Shakeshaft   David m Emma Norberry   Alan m Ruth   Ian m Janet

John Mark   Marianne   Victoria   Jessica   Lynne   Steven   Michael

age of sixteen years one half penny; from every covenanted servant man sixpence, and from every servant maid fourpence.

Item. There is due at the feast of Easter for every Stone Coalt foald in the said parish, Two Pence, and for every mare colt one penny.

Item. There is likewise due at the feast of Easter for every sheep sold between sheering time and Michaelmas ensuing a penny, and between Michaelmas and Easter following, or till the sheering time, two pence.

Item. There is due for every calf reared a half penny, for every calf killed or sold Three pence.

Item. There is due at the said Feast of Easter from every person exercising or possessing any Trade at any time four pence.

Item. There is due from every mill in the said Parish six shillings and eight pence to be paid at Easter.

Item. Hay, Clover etc. pay tithes in Grass Cocks.

Item. Wool pay tithe the day of sheering the sheep.

Item. There is due for every calf cow, one shilling or six pounds of dry rind cheese, which may be sold at or adjudged by honest persons to be worth a shilling.

Item. There is due from every farrow cow (that is a cow not having calved that year) the sum of sixpence, or three pounds of dry rind cheese, which is valued at six pence.

Item. Pigs pay Tithe when fit to live from their dame.

Item. Eggs pay tithe, two for every hen, and three for every Cock.

Item. There is due at Easter for Registering of burials, six shillings and 8d.

Item. Flax, Hemp, Apples, Hops, Geese etc. pay tithe.

Kennexstone farm accounts from 1774

Amongst my family records is the farm account book of my ancestor Rowland Rogers who farmed at Kennexstone from the 1750s. The accounts book begins in 1774 and finishes in 1784. Included here are some extracts from the book in Rowland Rogers' handwriting.

The account that Rowland Rogers kept of the work done by William Jone in the year 1775, including liming and dunging the fields, and working on the harvest. Rowland Rogers also 'had in the harvest 9 pints of ale.'

On the 23rd August, Rowland Rogers agreed to pay David Harry three pounds a year, and kept a record of how much he had been advanced throughout the year. The deductions include 11 shillings for going to Swansea fair and bull bait, and 6d for attending a cockfight. He also paid 12 shillings to Richard Punner, who on the land tax records for 1780 is recorded as living at Old Muzzard. He married Sarah Rogers in 1767.

The record that Rowland Rogers kept of the work done by Marrish Richard in 1777 is shown below. Besides reaping and thrashing wheat, carrying hay and cutting furze, he has yoked the oxen (Silk and Silver), and delved the gardens.

Rowland Rogers kept a record between 1784 and 1786 of when his cows went to the bull.

Below is an account of 'what was had of William Hullin in ye year 1775, for trimmins.' William Hullin is recorded as living at Barraston on the land tax records.

Rowland Rogers kept this account of the number of sheep he has sheared from 1779-1782.

In 1785, Rowland Rogers makes the following agreement with Elinor Evan:

Rowland Rogers agreed with Elinor Evan the 30th Day of August 1785, for £2 12s a year to be his covenant servant til the 30th Day of August 1786. He makes a deduction of 2s 6d when she goes to Rocilly Mapsant, and of 10s 6d when she went to Penrice 'fayer'.

Amongst his many other accounts, Rowland Rogers records that a whittle costs 6d, and he makes a deduction of 1s 6d for a day off for St. Steven's Day. He paid Marrish Richard 6d a day for 'rootling furs', and 19s 6d for 'quaring of stones and keeping ye kiln at Cheriton wod.' In 1777, Ann William had 9s for getting 'Hundred and for sheaves of reed in'.

'Fayers' are mentioned in Penrice, Llanrhidian and Swansea, 'cokfites' in 'Llanmadock' and Porteynon, and mapsants – an annual festival commemorating the patron saint of the parish – in Lake and 'Rocilly'.

'Leyshon Rogers made an agreement with Jane Omphrey for £2 5s a year, and the year to begin the 8th Day of April 1784, and to be free at any Quarter if he do not like her, or shee like him.'

In his book *West Gower*, 1885, the Rector of Llanmadoc, the Rev. J. D. Davies, writes of a manuscript – a commonplace book written by Leyshon Rogers of Llangennith – that 'came into his hands.' The book begins in 1784, and the land tax and parish records of Llangennith in 1784 confirm that the only Rogers family recorded in the parish of Llangennith on that date is that of Rowland Rogers, Kennexstone, whose son Leyshon – born in 1752 – made the above agreement in 1784 with Jane Omphrey.

Leyshon Rogers married Ruth Clement on the 29th October 1788, and died on the 4th November 1834, aged 82.

The following extracts from Leyshon Rogers's manuscript are given, as in the original *West Gower* book, without any alteration.

January 1st 1784, the great frost and snow began, and held till February the 21st, which is 5 weeks before it came to change, there was some snow till the 5th March before it went clear off.

The frost began the 7th day of December in the year 1784, came to rain the third day of February in the year 1785. Saturday the 18th day of December in the year 1784 was the most dangerous time that was ever remembered in any age by any living person that is living, some horses lost their lives, and the turnpike roads was all in a plate of ice.

From the 18th day of February 1785, there was no rain of any value till the 1st day of June that was three months and most three weeks, and after that it was very dry, till the beginning of September, and then there was so much rain that the late corn was all most lost, that the corn groud fast to the ground, and some was carried off the ground that could not be bound.

January the 6th in the year 1786 there was so much water upon the face of the ground as was ever seen by any age now living. Coome Kiln was every bit under water that it ran along the road towards Burry.

Leyshon Rogers notes that the customary price for making hay is 2d and 3d a day in 1787. Masons were paid 1s a day, but upon their own meat 1s 6d; Joiners were paid 8d a day, and Coopers 10d, and that a farmer 'may give a miller 15s a year, and have it ground towll free, and to have it weighed in and out, only to allow one pound for waste.'

Alluding to the practice of cockfighting, which was very prevalent at that time and long after, he says:

"John Bevan had for the cockfight the gun that Leyshon Rogers had."

He mentions the purchase of property by Mr. Lucas. Mr. Lucas bought July 6th 1776, the two farms, Hardins down, and the farm at Llangennith of Mr. Bennet Dosset for £505. The farm at Hardins down was 24 acres and that at Llangennith 13 acres.

Among a variety of memorabilia, there is one in respect of witches and headed as follows:

"For the art of unwitching, or unlucky people, the fable I heard, so that I wrote –

If you think that you have any thing that is witched, take some may Tree and beat what ever cattle or any thing that you think is witched all over first, and boil some of the may tree in milk, then give them two hornfulls for some few days, till the witch comes to say God bless them.

If a witch be coming to the door, take a birch broom and put it a cross in the door, then the witch cannot come into the house till the broom be tuk out of the door."

Leyshon Rogers also writes of a toll called a 'Toll Pixey'. Rev. J. D. Davies identifies this toll as an ancient tribute paid to the Duke of Beaufort and collected by his steward. In the 1780s, this would have been Gabriel Powell. 'The toll pixey that Mr. Powell do use is 4d per £ for every pound's wort of the crop that is took.'

A great portion of Mr. Rogers' book is filled up with various recipes for the ailments of cattle and horses, remedies and treatment of cuts, bruises and complaints incidental to man or beast. At the time, there was no medical man in Gower. The first resident medical practitioner was Mr. Daniel Davies, surgeon of Reynoldston, who first came into Gower about the year 1816.

The Rev. J. D. Davies records that one part of the manuscript contains a collection of poetical compositions suitable for Valentines, and gives some examples.

'You are the one and only one,
And I am only he,
That doth love one and only one,
And you, my dear, is she.'

'My dear and better, pray read this letter,
And on the writer some pity take,
You may have richer – but not have better,
I could my dear, die for your sake.'

'The ring is round, and hath no end,
So is my love for you my friend,
The rose is read, and vilates blue,
Carnations sweet and so are you.'

'Streams of pleasure, rivers of wine,
Plantations of tea, and a young girl to my mind.'

Leyshon Rogers records some of the remarkable occurrences of the time. He writes of the many cattle that died in 1782 for the want of food –

". . . fodder was so scarce that the thatch of the houses was given to the animals to eat."

"On the 4th May 1782, people are obliged take the thatch from their houses to give to their cattle for want of fodder."

"May the 13th 1782, there were 54 hides on a market day, of cattle that died for want of fodder."

Although the price of meat in the late 18th Century was exceedingly low, game was rather an expensive item:

"The first of the season the woodcocks is seven shillings and six-pence a brace. A Hare is one shilling and sixpence, and pattridge is sixpence each. A wild duck is one shilling and three pence each, and teal is nine pence each."

It seems from an entry in the book that it was the custom to white-wash the church once a year:

"There is a 7s 6d allowed by the parish for white washing the church every year, and 2s 6d for white washing the chancel every year. There is 1d per load allowed by the parish for carring every load of lime into the church. For every ladder that is Borrowed for the use of the church, the owner may charge 2d per day for it, have been paid by the Church Wardens. There is 2d per load allowed by the Parish for fetching sand for the church."

Tiles are quoted at the time 10s a thousand; a two-year-old steer was worth £2 15s. Leyshon Rogers writes of selling a pair in St. Andrew's fair in Penrice for £5 10s.

J. D. Davies brings his choice of extracts from the book to a close with a collection of recipes which he hopes that by the "quaintness of the verbiage will amuse, if the remedies do not benefit his readers."

For the shortness of Breath is to make Tea with the blossom of coults foot sweetened with treacle.

For the heart burning is one bean dried very hard, to eat this will stop it soon.

For the Blast, mix flowr and woter together and drink it as soon as possible.

For a cut, poun parsly and butter together and drink it as soon as possible.

For a boyl, take white Bread and butter together and chaw it and spread it on a Cloth and put it on it.

For a Could, take Water and boil it, then put in Rosemary into it in a Jug, then let the person hould it over the Jug and then cover his head with a whittel til comes to sweat, then go to bed as fast as possible and keep warm is very good.

For a strain for a Cristian, take hogs lard and Brockley powned together, and put to it is very good.

If any person burn himself, to rub soap in it is very good.

For the shortness of Breth and heft in the Stomeg, take Brimstone powdered and Honey and mix in a glass of Brandy. Drink it in the morning fasting, and rest one morning.

For to stop Bleeding at the Nose on any person is to take the moss from the White Thorn and put it in your Noster hole will stop it.

To keep of any Disorder from any person and make ye Blood to Surkylate, is to take 1 quart of Decoction of Bark and to mix 1 pint of Brandy with it, and then to drink a glass full every night and morning fasting, so long as it do hould.

The oil of time is very good for the toothake, one drop of it is enough at one time on a bit of lint is a present cure you put it to your tooth.

For a bruise or strip on man or beast is to mix Viniger and flower together and make a plaster of it, the white wine viniger is the best.

The 'Cambrian' Newspaper

The *Cambrian* newspaper was published every Friday in Swansea from 1804 throughout the 19th century. The Rogers family of Kennexstone are mentioned four times between 1825 and 1853.

The marriage of Mr. John Rogers, Kennexstone, to Catherine, third daughter of the late Mr. George Beynon, Burry Green, is announced on the 11th June 1825, and only one year later, the newspaper records the death of Catherine, aged 30, just thirteen days after her confinement.

On the 15th May 1841, the marriage is reported at Llangennith Church by the Rev. Samuel Phillips, of Mr. George Beynon of the Welcome to Town, Llangennith, to Mrs. Eliza Rogers, widow of Mr. Leyshon Rogers, Kennexstone.

On the 23rd September 1853 an auction of the crop and stock of George Beynon is advertised.

TO BE SOLD BY AUCTION,
By Mr. EVAN JONES,
At KNIXTONE FARM in the Parish of Llangenith Gower,
on WEDNESDAY, 12th OCTOBER, 1853,
THE STOCK and CROP, the property of Mr.
G. BEYNON,
Credit will be given on all sums above £1 10s.
Sale to commence at eleven o'clock in the forenoon.

My father's family, Kennexstone.
Grandmother Elizabeth Rogers, Minnie, Grandfather John Rogers, John and Olive.

My mother's family, from Barraston, Gower.
Grandad George Jones, John Jones, Grandma Mary Jones, Evan Jones, Greta and Gladys Jones.
Missing from the family photo is Trevor Jones who was serving in the army in the First World War.

During the First World War, a large house in Horton was converted into a hospital for wounded soldiers. Many Gower women enrolled as V.A.D. nurses in the hospital, including my mother Gladys Jones (later Rogers), and my aunt Minnie Rogers (later Jones).

My mother Gladys is the first nurse seated on the right, my aunt Minnie is next to her.

GOWER CHURCH MAGAZINE, NOVEMBER 1917.

Red Cross Hospital, Horton.

Gifts received – Game, fruit and vegetables – Miss Talbot. Apples – Miss Roberts, Ilston. Fruit & vegetables from the various Harvest Festivals, including 68 eggs from Llanrhidian.

The Nurses on duty at present are: Miss Lloyd, Miss Minnie Rogers, and Miss G. Jones. There are twelve patients in Hospital at present – Lily Edwards, Quartermaster and Lady Superintendent.

Soldiers and nurses at Horton. Gladys Jones (later Rogers) standing on right.

Mrs. Gladys Rogers

During her recorded conversation with an archivist at St. Fagan's, Mrs. Gladys Rogers recalled the food she had helped to prepare for a Gower 'Bidding Wedding'.

I remember helping to make mutton pies for a bidding wedding. These weddings were popular in Gower. The couple would send a man to invite guests to their wedding with a rhyme. The family of the bride would kill a sheep – or ask a local farmer to kill one – and two days before the wedding, four or five women neighbours would go to the bride's house to help prepare the pies. We would line a milk tin with pastry; the mutton would be minced and placed in the tin with onions and seasoning, then covered with pastry and baked. The wedding celebration would be held in the bride's home. The guests would be offered a small piece of cold pie and were then expected to make a contribution of 5-10 shillings. This was to help the young couple set up home. The 'Bidder' kept an account of how much was given by each guest, and the wedding couple were expected to return the favour when they were invited to a wedding. The guests would be offered beer to drink, and later there would be dancing. The last bidding wedding I remember was in the early 1900s, and was held in a barn – both the lunch and the dancing.

Mrs. Vera Thomas, the daughter of Mrs. Gladys Rogers, remembers that this would have been the last bidding wedding in Gower, when George Nicholas of Hardings Down married Margaret Ann Tucker of Old Henllys in Llandewi Church.

GOWER CHURCH MAGAZINE, PARISH OF LLANDEWI. MARCH 1906

Vicar and Rector: Rev. John Hughes.

Marriage. Feb. 8. George Francis Nicholas, of Hardings Down, Llangennith to Margaret Anne Tucker of Old Henllys, Llandewi.

This marriage was looked forward to with great interest for some weeks prior to its celebration from the fact of it being a 'Bidding Wedding,' which is an old custom revived, but which had become almost obsolete, no marriage of its kind having for many years past taken place, so far as the writer is aware, in this part of the peninsula. In addition to the relatives and friends who attended the ceremony, and afterwards joined in the festivities, a great number came for miles around to see the bridal procession. Unfortunately, though they made every effort to enter the Church, they did not succeed in doing so, as it was more than full when they arrived. Another reason for the great interest in this marriage was the popularity of the bride. She was a special favourite both in and out of the parish. She was a communicant and a Sunday School Attendant. But it was in her home that she was most beloved, by parents, brothers and sisters, each of whom will miss her sadly for her thoughtfulness and unselfishness, and especially for her usefulness in assisting in the management of the house and their large and young family. Surely her parents are to be sympathised with in losing such a

George and Margaret Ann Nicholas, née Tucker,
outside Llangennith Church on the 50th Anniversary
of their Bidding Wedding.
(Photograph by kind permission of Susan and Phillip Nicholas).

daughter, and her husband to be congratulated in winning such a wife. We wish them a long and happy married life. The ceremony was partly choral, and Miss Wheeler came and presided at the Harmonium.

Bethesda Chapel, Burry Green

In February 1813, Diana, Baroness Barham left her ancestral home in Kent and visited Swansea. She met the Rev. Mr. Kemp, minister of the Countess of Huntingdon's chapel, who often preached in Gower. She travelled with him around the peninsula and became very concerned at the spiritual destitution of the people.

Bethesda Chapel, Burry Green.

Nine months later, Lady Barham returned to Gower and settled at Fairy Hill, a mansion in beautiful surroundings near Burry Green.

Lady Barham was the only daughter of Sir Charles Middleton, First Lord of the Admiralty, and on his death in 1813 had inherited both his

William Griffiths,
'The Apostle of Gower'.

Lady Barham.

title and a considerable fortune. As a committed Christian, she set about using her inheritance to help dispel the darkness she had found in Gower. A few Christian believers were preparing to set up a small meeting house on the edge of the Green. When she found that she and they held views in common, she asked if they would allow her to erect a considerably larger building and a manse as well. This was to be Bethesda Chapel as we now know it.

Having settled at Fairy Hill, Lady Barham contacted the Association of Calvinistic Methodists to find an evangelist for Gower. William Griffiths, employed by Lady Barham, came first to Penclawdd and then to Cheriton. In 1824, he was ordained and, under the patronage of Lady Barham's son, he became the resident minister at Burry Green where he remained until his death in 1861.

Lady Barham attended services at Bethesda Chapel, carried from Fairy Hill in a sedan chair, as she was often unwell. She had her own small room adjoining the chapel, with a fire and a 'stable' door opening at the top so that she could join in the worship but withdraw if necessary.

She continued to use her wealth to help the poor people of Gower and often paid their doctor's bills. Once a young girl came with a request for the doctor. Lady Barham asked in exasperation, "What did you do before I came?" The young girl replied, "Please, my lady, we died."

Glyn Rogers

My family has always worshipped in Bethesda Chapel, Burry Green. My father was its Secretary for many years, and every Sunday I would walk to the Chapel with him half an hour before the service began, in order to light the oil lamps. He was the conductor of a joint choir that was formed by Burry Green and Llangennith chapels, and as the hymn-books were in solfa, well-attended solfa classes were held in the chapel. Dean Gordon, who has been the organist at the chapel for over seventy years recalls that before the arrival of the organ, the singing was un-accompanied – the tune being pitched by a 'Precentor' with a tuning fork. The chapel organ arrived in 1910 amid great controversy – a retired sea captain who lived at Stembridge House didn't believe in worship-ping God by machinery!

I enjoyed the Sunday school classes, and once a year came the Sunday school trip. The trip was not just for the children – everybody in the village would come. We looked forward to it all year. One workman would have to stay behind on the farm to care for the stock, and we would go off to a different place each year – Ilfracombe by boat was a favourite!

A small boy and a big cap – on a Sunday school boat trip to Ilfracombe with my parents. Also in the photograph are Mrs. Tanner and Gladys Tanner, Stembridge.

A Burry Green Chapel celebration. Included here are my parents,
Jack the Lane, Minnie and Olive.

The wedding of my sister Vera to Cecil Thomas in 1951,
when the chapel was still lit by oil lamps.
The Rev. Medford Lloyd officiated, and my uncle
Emlyn Rogers was the organist.

54

Outside the Manse, Burry Green on the day of David's christening.
From left – Rev. Tudor Lloyd, Mrs. Evans, Glyn, Christopher, Ivy,
Olive Rogers (holding David), and Dean Gordon.

Rev. Tudor Lloyd came to Burry Green Chapel in 1956. On the 13th April 1994, I was chairman when the members of the three chapels of the North Gower Pastorate – Burry Green, Cheriton and Old Walls – met to make a presentation to him on the occasion of his retirement. The Rev. Lloyd was presented with a reclining chair, a painting, and two cheques for Durtlang Hospital, Assam.

In 1958, the Rev. Lloyd had drawn our attention to the urgent need for trained doctors and medical staff in Assam. The chapels started a Medical Missionary Fund, and people from the local Gower villages made contributions. We chose a young Indian student, Mr. Biakmawia, to support. He studied in Vellore Christian Medical School, and later came to the UK to continue his studies, and was able to visit us in Gower. One visit was planned just before Christmas, and the chapel members had received a tape of "Oh come, all ye faithful" in the Mizo language. A group of ladies learnt the carol phonetically and sang it for him. He was delighted and deeply moved. Mr. Biakmawia qualified as a doctor in 1966, and became the first paediatrician in his State. He is now the Medical Director of Durtlang.

The Rev. Tudor Lloyd has continued to live in Burry Green since his retirement. In Gower, he is held in affectionate esteem, and considered to be a friend to all.

Llanmadoc School

Llanmadoc School Football Team, circa 1910.
(By kind permission of Randolph Jenkins).

Like my father before me, I attended Llanmadoc School.

> LLANMADOC SCHOOL LOG BOOK 1914
> 'The school is taught in two rooms, the larger of which accommodates the Upper Dept. and the smaller, the Infant class.
> Owing to the difficulty of preventing sheep from entering the playground, the small plot for growing flowers for Nature Study has unfortunately had to be abandoned.'

My father passed an examination to go to the Grammar School in Swansea. He had to lodge in Swansea during the week, returning home on the weekends.

> SCHOOL LOG BOOK, 15TH FEBRUARY 1905
> 'Received a letter from the clerk informing us that Elizabeth Dix, Bovehill, and John Rogers, Kennexstone, passed satisfactorily in Standard V.'

When I was at school, at playtime we boys would go out on the moor, and we would ride the donkeys there. We lost all track of time! Polly Beynon, our teacher, would come out to where we were playing, loudly ringing the school bell. As soon as the boys saw her, they would cut up through the fields before she could catch them and would be sitting quietly at their desks by the time that she had returned to the classroom.

Polly had a large stove in the classroom on which she would warm up her dinner. She would send boys down to the well to fetch water. They would often add a good handful of tadpoles to the water, and when Polly tried to pour the water from the kettle, none would come out, as the spout would be blocked with tadpoles.

In the 1930s, seventeen whales were washed ashore on Whitford Sands. Our teachers took us to see them, and as it was a long walk to the beach, we had a whole day off school.

> School Log Book, 8th May 1934
> 'The beach at Llanmadoc, having been visited by a school of Sea Monsters, the upper class children in charge of Miss Thomas, visited the beach to view same.'

The school closed on the 11th October 1935, and all the children were transferred to Llanrhidian School. I used to travel there by bus. There was a two-bus garage in Llangennith, and the drivers and conductors would drive past our house in their cars or on motorbikes, on the way to start their morning shift. I would enjoy travelling with them to pick up the bus at Llangennith, and one morning Wilfred Winch stopped to pick me up in a brand new Ford 8, which, he told me proudly, had cost £100.

I later went to Clevedon College in Swansea, and then did a course in Pencoed Agricultural College before returning to Gower to work on the farm with my father.

In 1985, on the 50th Anniversary of the demolition of the school, a reunion was held on the site. Many of its former pupils travelled to Llanmadoc to meet old friends and remember their schooldays.

When I was sixteen, I went with some friends to a carnival in Llangennith. A little while later I was feeling quite ill, with a very sore throat. Dr. Moreton was not available, so a young doctor that we hadn't seen before called by. He was concerned as he thought I had a serious infection, but when Dr. Moreton called in later he said I had tonsillitis and it would do me good to go out into the fresh air. I grew steadily worse, and my throat was very painful, but fortunately the young doctor came back as he had been worrying about me. He realised that I

57

Folk dancers of Llanmadoc School, 1932.
Glyn Rogers, 2nd row, third from right.
Our teacher Miss Thomas seen here on the right, used to ride to school on her motorbike.
Included in this photograph are – centre back row – Joe Taylor, Doreen Bevan.
Front row – Nina Beynon, Vera Rogers, Heather Morris & Ivy Davies.
(By kind permission of Randolph Jenkins).

Whales at Llanmadoc, May 1934.

had diphtheria and asked if I could bear the pain if he made an incision in my throat.

I was glad that he was able to do something, so with a swab of iodine he went ahead. I was then rushed to hospital. When I was recovering, the sister of the ward told me, "That doctor saved your life!" – but I never saw him again to thank him.

With the exception of my father, the whole family went down with diphtheria. My father had to sleep in a barn whilst the house was fumigated. The cause of the infection was traced to a girl who was employed on the farm – she was a carrier, and did not catch the disease herself.

After eight weeks in hospital, I returned home. The family in the meantime had moved from the old house into Bryn View, so I came straight from hospital into my new home. The nurses in the hospital became great friends – I even wrote a poem about them all, and they would come down to Kennexstone on holiday.

Included here are Gwynne Richards, Dean Gordon, Megan Price, Gladys Hughes, Clive Jenkins, the Rev. Tudor Lloyd, Glyn Rogers and Rev. Herbert Nicholas.
(By kind permission of the *South Wales Evening Post*).

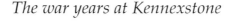

The war years at Kennexstone

Although I was called up and had a medical ready to join the army, I received a letter saying that, as agriculture was so important, I was needed on the farm. I joined the Home Guard, and we once went on manoeuvres with American soldiers in Penrice. We later lined up to get our food, and were impressed with the meat and vegetables that we were served. Unfortunately, we then had pudding and custard piled on the same dish. We had to look under the custard to find the potatoes. We also went on an expedition to try to reach Swansea docks, but I was 'taken prisoner' in Sketty, and had to wear a white armband.

The Home Guard units of Llanrhidian, Llanmadoc and Llangennith planned a combined exercise to launch an attack on the Wireless station on Rhossili Down. The soldiers manning the post were warned that an attack would take place. After a few pints at the King's Head, the Llan-gennith boys decided to attack from the sea, which meant a precipitous climb – difficult enough in daylight, but the raid was carried out at night! It was quite a scramble up the hill – we fell into rabbit holes lost our hats and equipment – but eventually reached the top. The soldiers were guarding the other side of the hill, which was being attacked by the Llanrhidian and Llanmadoc boys, who were soon captured. The Llangennith boys cut the fence and reached the post. I believe there were a few sackings after our success!

The Ministry of Agriculture would tell us what crops we were to grow on the farm. During the war, because of the lack of farm workers, a lorry would arrive from Swansea Prison with prisoners who were accompanied by two warders. They would help us on the land. Later, we had two German prisoners-of-war – Bruno and Siegfried. They would come over from the camp in Scurlage. They were both strong boys, and could carry two hundred weight bags of phosphate without effort. They were full of energy, and would do double somersaults in the fields. Not long ago, Siegfried called here with his wife and reminisced about the meals he had enjoyed around our kitchen table. We also had two land girls – Pat and Nancy – who helped us on the farm.

The Norbury family were evacuated to our farm when their father, Fred, was posted to the Orkney Isles. Originally from Southampton, Mrs. Norbury and her four children came to stay for the duration of the war, but never returned home. They settled in this area, and Ken, one of their sons, is now the father-in-law of my son, David.

We saw quite a few plane crashes around here. A delivery driver who worked for the 'Home and Colonial' was driving in a van near to Burry when he saw a plane crash into a nearby field. The Polish pilot climbed

The Norbury family, from left: Mrs. Norbury, Beryl, Vera, Ken, Mr. Norbury, Gwen and Gerald.

Llangennith, Llanmadoc and Llanrhidian Home Guard Units.
Back row from left – Stanley Gordon, Lenny Jeffreys, Glyn Rogers, Gerwyn Nicholas,
William Taylor, Alan Gwyn, David Bevan, Reg Eaton, others unknown.
2nd row – Walter Beynon, Jack the Lane, Tucker Beynon, ? , Ernie Rees, Gwyn Lewis,
Will Davies, others unknown.
3rd row – Ronald Winch, Rev. Ben Jones, ?, Col. Helme, ?, ?, Dr. Moreton, Rev. Jones Evans.
Front row – Cliff Jenkins, Stanley Dunn, John Jones, Gerald Sullivan.
(By kind permission of Miss Audrey John).

out uninjured, and the driver took him safely back to Fairwood. The first attack on Swansea Docks took place on a Sunday night. I saw a plane involved in the attack coming over our farm, flying very low with a swastika on its side. It was just cresting the hedges, and I could see the pilot clearly; he was trying to avoid the radar. I saw another plane chased by fighters; it dropped two bombs on the Pancross and two on the common at Kennexstone, leaving a crater. The plane was eventually shot down.

A Beaufighter came down in Tyle House field – it had just taken off from Pembrey and was heading for Fairwood. Some RAF personnel were sent to guard it. They had to wait until a 'Queen Mary' – a 60ft. articulated truck – came to pick the plane up. The men came up to our farm for cups of tea and a rest between their shifts.

There was a collision just after the war when a Vampire Fighter hit the tail of a Meteor Fighter. The Meteor crashed in Broadway field just above Muzzard, and the pilot bailed out successfully. The other pilot managed to return safely to Fairwood Aerodrome.

During the war years, we had double summertime. My neighbour Sid Tucker came to ask me if I would help him carry his hay. We couldn't start too early as the dew was on the field until midday. We eventually left the field at one o'clock in the morning. His wife asked him when we were coming in for supper, as she would soon be getting everyone else's breakfast!

There was of course some black market dealing going on in the war years. Joe Williams, the butcher in Llangennith, had just slaughtered a pig when he had a phone call to tell him that an inspector was heading towards his home. Joe told his wife to get into bed, and wrapping the pig's carcase in cloth, he put it into bed alongside her. The inspector checked all the rooms of the house, even going into the bedroom, as Joe had told him that his wife was ill with the flu. The inspector beat a hasty retreat when he saw steam rising from the bed!

'The Happiest Days of Your Life', 1955

In the 1950s, The Young People's Guild met every Friday night in the vestry at Old Walls, and every year, under the guidance of the Rev. Medford Lloyd, we would perform a play in all the local village halls.

Edna Jenkins, Glyn Rogers, George Richards & Betty Clement.

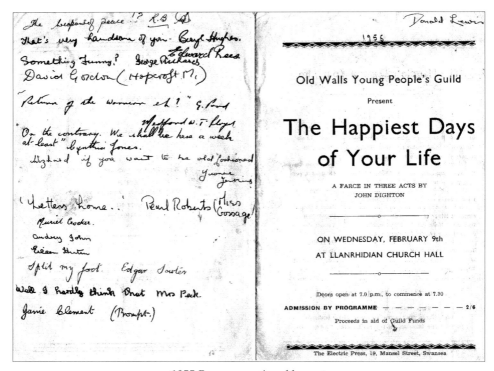

1955 Programme signed by cast.
(By kind permission of Donald Lewis).

I would transport the cast and scenery in a lorry belonging to Donald Lewis's father, Weobley Castle. We had some enjoyable times and some worrying moments when lines were forgotten or cues missed. We became experts at keeping a conversation going until we were back on track. The plays were very popular – we would perform to packed halls in Gower.

During our rehearsals, we took it in turns to make the tea. One night it was the turn of Alex Brockie. He arrived with a large teapot; the tea in it was so thick it was a job to pour it. "Well, Alex," queried the Rev. Medford Lloyd, "what have you done to this tea?"

"My mother always says one for each person and one for the pot," replied Alex, "so I have put in twenty-two teaspoonfuls!"

I met my wife Ivy at a dance in Llanrhidian Church Hall. The dances there were well attended. The vicar, the Rev. Ben Jones and Sidney Williams used to be on the door to take the entrance money. There would always be a group playing at the dance, and young people would go to Llanrhidian from all over Gower.

The Bandits were one group that played at the hall, and we had 'Old Tyme Dancing' with the Jenkins family. Our local musician was Ron Parry who had his own band and played the accordion.

Ron Parry and accordion.
(By kind permission of Mrs. Jean Tucker).

The wedding of Glyn and Ivy Rogers, 1954.

Four generations of the Rogers family.
Elizabeth Rogers (holding Christopher), with John and Glyn Rogers.

GOWER MEMORIES

Glyn Rogers at the Gower Show.

I remember my father telling me that when there were no dentists here, the blacksmith in Llanmadoc would pull teeth. He recalled seeing one man running through Cheriton with the blacksmith behind him in hot pursuit.

"What's wrong?" he asked the blacksmith.

The blacksmith replied that the man wanted to have a tooth pulled, but had lost his nerve, adding, "I have to catch him or he'll ruin my reputation!"

My grandfather was very strict about observing the Sabbath. My father wasn't even allowed to shave on Sundays. He would sneak down to the river, and when out of sight of the farm, have a shave in the water where he could see his reflection.

The only work done on the farm on Sundays in my grandfather's day was feeding the stock. The animals' food would be prepared in buckets on Saturday afternoon – there was no fetching hay on Sundays!

*A Gower wedding celebration. On the 23rd August 1904, Minnie Rogers,
aged 10 of Kennexstone attended the wedding of William Tucker, Parc y Rhedin,
to Sophia Anne Davies of Landimore. Minnie is the young girl on the left of this photograph.*

My mother remembered travelling to Swansea by horse bus. The bus would carry about twelve people – two had to travel outside. It would take about three hours to reach Swansea, and the passengers would have to get out and walk up all the hills on the way.

One old boy would occasionally take too much to drink at a local pub, but his faithful horse would always take him safely home in his cart to Landimore. Some boys decided to play a trick on him, and when he went inside to sleep it off, they let the horse out of the shaft, and put the cart on the other side of the gate. They then put the cart shafts through the gate and re-harnessed the horse to the cart. The old boy woke up in a bit of a daze, and went out to check on his horse. He couldn't work out what was wrong, so went indoors to fetch a saw, and proceeded to saw through the shafts!

When the men went about their work, they were always whistling or singing. People seemed a lot happier then.

Miss Stephens lived in Kennexstone Cottage, where she kept geese. I walked past one day and thought they looked a bit odd. She came out to ask if there was something wrong. "Your geese look a bit strange," I told her. They were all wearing cardigans that she had knitted for them, because as she said, "They feel the cold, too!"

Walter Tanner and his son Wally lived in Llangennith. I remember Gwyn Lewis telling me that he was in his yard one day when Wally walked in. It was a bitterly cold day, and Gwyn invited Wally in for a cup of tea, and they spent quite a while chatting in front of the fire. After half an hour, Gwyn said to Wally, "I don't see you often, Wally, was there something special that you wanted?"

"Well," said Wally, "I'll tell you what it is. My father went up a ladder onto the roof of Llangennith Church, and the ladder broke. He's stuck up on the roof, and told me to come over to you and borrow a ladder!"

Gwyn Gordon told me that he had had great difficulty in getting the money that he was owed from one man. He would go to Gowerton Mart, as this man was always there on a Tuesday, but as soon as he saw Gwyn he would get into a crowd of men, and Gwyn couldn't get near him. Eventually, Gwyn wrote him a letter asking for payment. He had a reply by return of post. The man wrote that he had his milk cheque on the 23rd of the month, and then he would put all the bills that were awaiting payment into a hat. Those that he drew out would be paid. However, he informed Gwyn, that having received his 'nasty' letter, Gwyn's bill would *not* be going into the hat next month!

Old Dr. Moreton was our doctor. I remember him coming here one day still laughing about a conversation he had had with John Taylor, Delvid. "What's wrong with thee, John?" he had asked. "That's for thee to find out," replied John. "If my cow's bad, and I call the vet, the cow can't tell him what's wrong with her!"

If we could hear the trains going up Llanelli way, we always had good weather, but if we could hear Llandewi church bell ringing, then rain would not be far away.

I was helping Phil Bowen one day to hoe swedes. I wanted to leave the field to shake my hay. Phil growled crossly, "See those white horses over Worm's Head? That means that there'll be rain by the next day." I reluctantly stayed to help him, but the next morning Phil was right – it rained all day!

69

David Morgan's lorry at The Gower Show, circa 1920s. His stores were in Reynoldston,
and supplied all the local farmers with their equipment.
(By kind permission of Robert Jones, Knelston).

Years ago, before lorries came to Gower, coal had to be brought by horse and cart from Llanmorlais. One farmer went to Llanmorlais to fetch coal for the local vicar, and carefully loaded into the vicar's coal-house. "Thank you, my man," said the vicar, "The Lord will repay you."

"But," replied the farmer, "I'd rather *thee* would!"

The first Gower Show was held at Penrice in 1906, and has been held annually ever since. It was an important date in the calendar of Gower farmers, and the schoolchildren in Llanmadoc would be given a day's holiday to attend the show.

Jack the Lane went to St. Fagan's on a trip with a party from Llangennith. He went into Kennexstone Farmhouse, and sat down on a settle by the kitchen table. "I'm sorry, sir, you're not allowed to sit there," a guide told him.

Jack replied, "I've sat here for many meals, and you – nor anybody else – are not going to move me from here!"

On hearing this, the guide invited him to share his memories of the farmhouse.

There was a certain gravedigger in Gower who wasn't "quite the weight". He took a great pleasure in digging graves, so much so in fact that if he heard of anyone in his village that was very ill, he would be seen walking back and forth outside the house, spade over his shoulder, waiting for the bad news!

Sid Clement, Dunraven, was out ploughing the steep fields near Stembridge. Jack of Western Mill came by and shouted to him. Sid thought that he wanted to tell him something important so he stopped his tractor. When he found that Jack had just been passing the time of day with him, and that he was now unable to restart his tractor, he said sternly to Jack, "Never stop me again unless there's death about!"

Sid and I would help each other out with the thrashing. One bitterly cold day we were all wrapping sacks around our shoulders to keep warm. Sid said to me, "I don't know what you are all making such a fuss about – you know nothing about the cold! When I was in the navy in the First World War, we were in one place that was so cold that if you spit, it would freeze before it hit the ground and hop back at you!

Gower Show, 1939.
From right – George Brynley Hughes, seated in front is George Nicholas, Gwyn Lewis,
Reggie Jenkins, Muzzard, George Taylor, Vanguard Buses, ?,
Romney Williams, Glyn Hughes, ? .
(By the kind permission of Randolph Jenkins).

Sid Tucker was walking home from church with the vicar. The Queen had just opened the Severn Bridge. Mr. Moses, the vicar, told Sid that his son was taking him over the bridge on the following Thursday, and invited Sid to join them. Sid replied, "I don't know, man. Are you bound to go *this* Thursday?" The Vicar replied that it was his son's day off, so it would have to be Thursday. "What's the problem, Mr. Tucker?"

"Well," replied Sid, "I don't think I'll come. I'd rather letten set well first!"

I remember Eliza Thomas (Eliza Mog we called her), who kept the shop in Burry Green. I went in one morning early in the year, and said, "What lovely weather."

"Hang on you, boy," she replied. "We haven't had a blackthorn winter yet!"

This was when the white blackthorn blossom was in flower, covering the trees like snow.

George Tucker, Llangennith, was getting married and was having a house built by Walter and Wally Tanner. The wedding was getting close, but there was still a lot of work to do on it, so George went up to see if he could 'rush them along', but when he arrived at his unfinished house, he found Walter and Wally engrossed in a game of draughts. Time meant nothing to them!

Glyn James, Llanddewi, had three sons, and the boys always said he was a slave driver. They told me he would say to them, "Now, boys bach, go and cut some chaff whilst you have a spell," and "Now boys bach, do as much as you can today, we'll be busy tomorrow!"

When I was courting Ivy, I would drive back late in my car. One night, when I got to Llanrhidian, I was stopped by a flashing light. I braked the car and saw that it was P.C. Moon. "I thought it might be you," he said, and jumped into the car for a sit down and a cigarette!

Will Hopkins of 'Nottle' (North Hill) Farm took his tractor up to Oldwalls garage for Glanmor Williams for repairs. He intended catching the bus back home to the farm. Whilst he was there, Vivian Ace, the postman, came in with his new battery shaver, shaving himself as he walked in. Will was very impressed with this, and said, "I haven't had a shave for a couple of days. Will you shave me?" Vivian told him to sit down, and began to shave one side of his face clean, but then said, "I'll have to

A Valentine Day's Fancy Dress Dance in Llangennith Hall, 1946.

Back row, from left, Lyndon Grove, Terrence Beynon, Mike Tyrrell, Gwen Norbury, ?, ?, Val Jones, Barbara Howells, Ken Norbury, Marilyn Jones, Rosemary Tucker, Eric Gibbs, ?. 2nd Row – Valmai Williams, Vera Rogers, Miss Stephens, Mrs. Jones Evans, Rev. Jones Evans, Nina Beynon, Dora Nicholas, Dulcie Lewis, Mavis Williams. Front row – Gillian Rees centre.

(By kind permission of Mrs. Rosemary Tucker).

go now, I've got lots of letters to deliver. I'll call at your house, and shave the other side tomorrow." So poor Will had to get on the bus with only one side of his face clean-shaven.

I remember one autumn when I was baling in Burry Green; I had left my coat on the back of a tractor and went off to do another job. When I came back there was no sign of my coat – or my wallet. I looked everywhere, but couldn't find it, and remembering that I had seen a man around with not too good a character, I decided that he must have taken it. On Christmas Eve, as I was opening a small round bale of hay to feed the stock, I was surprised to see that my coat was inside it – shredded into pieces, but intact in the bale was my wallet and my money. What a Christmas present!

Mr. Gordon, Tyle House, took his bull to sell at Gowerton Mart. The bull went 'wicked' in the pen, and the auctioneer told Mr. Gordon that it was the wildest animal he had ever had in the mart. Mr. Gordon agreed with him, but he added, "It's a funny thing though. He's been brought up for three years next to Burry Green Chapel, and he ought to have known better!"

Gower Show, 1936. Dennis Jeffreys, Crickton, Llanrhidian, holding halter.

In springtime on a sunny morning, I would go down to the orchard and it would be like listening to the Hallelujah Chorus, as so many birds would be singing. There were always snipe and partridges around here – birds you don't see today. We also had barn owls and the swallows would nest in the barns, where the doors were so low that they would come flying out, missing you by inches.

I remember the tradesmen who would visit the farm. A cobbler from Morriston would call to repair our boots, John Richards a draper from Mansel Street would bring hard wearing farming clothes, and Thorn in Parkmill would take and recharge our wireless batteries.

I remember the time when my two uncles – Evan and John Jones, Barraston – used to graze sheep on Burry Holmes. The sheep would stay out there until they needed to be sheared. My uncles would then wait until low tide to bring them in. They would also fish there with long nets, often catching more herrings than they could carry.

My mother's cousin Reg worked at Barraston. He had a wonderful memory! He was having breakfast one morning when he said to his wife, "Glyn Rogers is seventy today!" When his wife asked him why he was so sure, he replied, "Because I had to make three trips on my bike to Kenning House to see if the baby had arrived, and on my third trip Glyn had been born!"

William John Davies used to act in the plays that our Young People's Guild would put on. He was a rent collector. I remember him telling us that he used to call to a house in Penclawdd in the hope of getting the rent money. He was never lucky enough to find the woman at home – her daughter always answered the door and told him her mother was out. One day, William spotted a pair of feet under a curtain at the bottom of the stairs. When the girl came out with the usual story, William told her, "Well, the next time that your mother goes out, tell her to take her feet with her!"

Gethin John, Ty'r Coed, drove a Wolseley 10. He later bought a Standard Vanguard from Gwyn Gordon. Gwyn had taken great care of this car, and I was surprised to see it a week later with dents in both wings.

"Well, boy," I said to Gethin, "What have you been doing with that car?"

"Trouble is," said Gethin, "It's a bit wider than the Wolseley, but if I keep this up, I'll soon get it the same size!"

Gower Show, 1933.
(By kind permission of Mrs. M. Davies, Knelston).

There were two retired spinster teachers – the Misses Price – who would ask Phil Bowen to do odd jobs for them. They asked him to do one job that they thought might be too difficult for him, but they needn't have worried, for as Phil told them, "There's only one job I can't do, and that's lay a fresh egg!"

Noah Rees, an old farmer from Penclawdd, was used to handling lambs, and checking if they were suitable for market. On the day of Penclawdd Carnival, a 'Best pair of legs' competition was held. The women who took part sat behind a curtain with only their legs showing, so that people could impartially choose the finest pair of legs. Noah didn't hesitate – he went straight up and began to 'handle the legs' as he would have done with his lambs. He chose the fattest pair, saying, "They handle the best!"

When I was very young, we went to a concert in Llangennith hall. There were very few cars about in those days, and Lenny Davies, Muzzard, kindly offered us a lift home in his car. When we got into the car he found that the lights had failed, so his brother lit a farm lantern that was in the boot of the car, and walked down the middle of the road all the way home, whilst we followed slowly behind in the car.

There is a field called Green Wells adjoining our land. There used to be a little cottage there, now in ruins, where 'Mog' Thomas, his wife Eliza and his daughter Dorothy lived. They were self-sufficient with a cow, a pig and some fowls.

AUTO-SUGGESTION
by Cyril Gwynn

I'll tell you a tale of Llanmadoc,
   Of Mog Thomas in his prime,
Of oxen and bidding weddings,
   'Way back in grandfather's time.

A wedding took place at Llanmadoc this day,
   To which Morgan intended to go,
But his boss gave orders to plough the ley,
   For he had some oats there to sow.

Morgan, of course, was bound to obey,
   'Though 'twas much against his grain,
And soon a scheme for getting away,
   Flashed into his crafty brain.

As to and from the oxen wend,
   He hatched this fine idea,
He said to the boss, as they turned on the end,
   "By gosh, thee'rt looking queer!"

"Oh," said the boss, "I'm feeling all right,
   There's nothing the matter with me,"
"Well," said Morgan, "thee'rt looking real white,
   There's something wrong I can see."

So every time they turned about,
   With many a blow and a curse,
Mog would exclaim, "Without a doubt,
   Gaffer, thee'rt getting worse."

The boss stuck this for a dozen turns,
   And then to Morgan he said,
"My legs feel shaky, my old head burns,
   Let out; I'll go home to bed."

Then as they were passing in by the styes,
    The missus was driving a sow in,
"Hullo, what's up?" she said in surprise,
    "I thought you both were out ploughing."

Then the gaffer began to explain,
    How sickly he felt and poorly,
Said he, "When a man is suffering pain,
    He can't keep on ploughing surely."

"My legs are all of a quaker,
    And my head is 'most fit to burst,
It came over me up in Long Acre,
    But 'twas Morgan noticed it first."

The good wife's tears were shedding,
    As she bade him come in to be nursed,
And Morgan went to the wedding,
    Because Morgan noticed it first.

My father used to tell me to do some hedging at 'Ned's House'. This area was half way up Grove Meadow on the left side of Kennexstone Common. It wasn't until years later that I realised that there were the ruins of a house there where 'Ned' must have lived.

In the 1841 census, Edward Rees (Ned), labourer, is recorded as living at Translake – the site of the old ruins.

Wally Tanner went into Swansea one evening, catching the last bus home at 10.20 p.m. Wally was an electrician, and found that the man that he was sitting beside on the bus was also one. They fell into an absorbing conversation – so much so that when the bus reached the man's stop in Killay, they were only half way through their chat, so Wally got off with him to finish it. He then started for Llangennith – a ten mile walk – but luckily met Gwyn Gordon at Cartersford, who was surprised to hear Wally's reason for such a long walk home.

His father Walter was just the same! He started a job in Emlyn Davies's house, Channel View, and Emlyn kept asking him to finish it. Walter arrived one night at a quarter to eleven, and said, "I've been worrying about not finishing the job, so I've come to do it now."

"But, Walter," they told him, "we're just going to bed."

"You go on," said Walter.

But they didn't sleep all night, as Walter was hammering in the attic until 3 a.m.

I remember my wife Ivy telling me about a couple living in Llan-yrnewydd, Penclawdd, who had twelve children. The wife went on a Mothers' Union trip, and asked her husband, as she would be late home, to make sure that the children were washed and in bed early. She arrived home, and asked how he had managed. He told her that he had had a bit of trouble with two of them, but couldn't remember which of his children were the troublesome ones. His wife went to check on the children and found that there were fourteen children in bed!

Scouts and Guides have camped in our fields since 1923.

The Ministry of Agriculture served me a notice that a field on Pen-mynydd would have to be cleared as it was infested with rabbits. Although the top field was dry, the lower field had to be drained. They arranged to bring a JCB in to dig the ditches. They dug down about 8-9 feet, and after the top layer had been removed, there were bands of colour, each band about a foot in depth – there was blue clay, and red and white sandstone amongst them. The JCB operator had never seen anything like it – and neither had we. It was like looking at a rainbow.

Sid Clement, Dunraven, remembered being in Llanmadoc School on the 27th June 1906, when there was an earth tremor. The master said, "Children, outside quickly!" Sid saw that the lamp that hung from the ceiling was swinging from side to side.

Jack and Gwyn the Lane only went to the King's Head, Llangennith, on Christmas Eve. Gwyn was telling me that he had to watch Jack, as the boys in the pub were trying to get him drunk. He said to Jack, "Come on, Jack boy, let's go through the door and get up home."

He replied, "What door, Gwyn?" Gwyn said, "That door over there!"

"Well, Gwyn, there's no door over there, but I'll tell thee what, next time I come round I'll go through –un!"

I remember the time that our neighbour Mr. New of Stormy Castle went into Swansea in his Land Rover. He was driving down the Kings-way when he saw the shop he needed on the other side of the road, so without stopping he drove straight over the central reservation. The headlines in the next day's *Evening Post* read "Cowboy on the Kingsway!"

When I was on the Community Council, I went to check on Mr. New as he was on our Electoral Roll, but found Councillor Taylor already there, as he was also on his Roll. On checking, we found out that the parish boundary passed straight through the centre of his house, so he was legally entitled to vote in both parishes.

During the 1950s, George Tucker, Llangennith, and I ran a yearly trip to London. We would leave Llangennith in the coach at 6.30 in the morning, and would arrive in London at 6 p.m. at night. There was no M4 in those days, so we would drive up through the Cotswolds. We stayed at the Royal Hotel, Russell Sq., where we had bed and breakfast for nine days. We also had two day trips to Brighton, Newmarket or Windsor – and all for princely sum of £8!

On one excursion out of London, we were approaching a busy road junction, with several roads meeting. The policeman on point duty stop-ped our bus, jumped aboard and started speaking Welsh. He was from Clydach, and said, "I couldn't let a United Welsh bus pass without seeing where they came from." There were lines of traffic held up in all directions.

The London trip.
Back row – Dennis Williams, Mrs. Bowen, George Tucker, driver, Mrs. Tucker,
Donald James, Mrs. Jones Evans & her son.
Elvet Bowen, ?, Jeff Behenna, ?, Glyn Rogers, Mike Tyrrell, Romney Williams, Gethin John.
Front – Cecil Thomas, Archie ?, Tom Thomas.

One year, seven local boys decided to drive to Blackpool in two cars. Donald Lewis, Weobley Castle, made all the arrangements, and took Gethin John, William Austin and Derek Jones in his car; Elved Bowen and Mike Tyrrell came in mine. After a stopover in Shrewsbury, we set off early for Blackpool, and had planned that because of road works, we needed to take a right turn. We then waited for the other car, but there was no sign of it. Now we had a problem, as only Donald knew where we were staying, though I did have a quick glance at the address. We decided to carry on to Blackpool, and stopped on the promenade to ask a policeman for help. He mentioned some of the areas in Blackpool, and one sounded familiar so we headed there and decided to call at all the hotels. I knocked at the first door, and was greeted by a woman who said, "You're early!" The first hotel we tried was the right one!

Donald and his group turned up 3½ hours later after a trip through the Mersey Tunnel.

From left – Derek Jones, Gethin John, Glyn Rogers,
William Austin and Donald Lewis.
(By kind permission of Cynthia Austin).

Kennexstone Cross was the meeting place on a Sunday night for all the young people in Gower. They would all walk over here to meet and have a chat. No work was done on the farms in Gower on a Sunday, but the day before we had cut our corn, but hadn't yet 'stooked' it. On the

Monday morning, we went into the field and found that the boys from Llanrhidian had made little ricks all over the field – but had put the heads facing outwards!

When I was young, we knew all the drivers of the Vanguard buses. If anyone needed anything in Swansea, they would come down to ask the drivers, and they would bring it back on the next trip. They made many trips to John Griffiths, the ironmongers in Union Street, Swansea, for us.

When the bus was waiting for its departure time in Swansea, boys would often come on board selling newspapers. An old man named Lenny Clement was sitting by his sister Greta, and he told the boy impatiently that he didn't want a paper. Greta said, "Why didn't thee buy one from the boy, we could use them for wrapping eggs?" Lenny changed his mind and bought two! This was in the days when eggs were packed individually – no special cartons in those days!

George Tucker was quite a character! He was our local bus driver. The buses in those days had a rail around the roof of the bus to hold baskets securely. The driver would climb up a ladder at the back of the bus, lower a rope for the baskets to be attached and pull it up with a hook.

1920 Vanguard Bus advertisement.

Glyn Rogers, George Tucker, and his Albion bus.

Colonel Helme of Hillend, Llangennith, used to send his laundry in a hamper to Swansea by bus. One day, Jack the Lane was the conductor, and the only person on board – so George did a few swerves to give him a bit of a fright. Jack rang the bell furiously, so George stopped the bus. He found that the Colonel's hamper had shot off the top of the bus, and his washing was spread all over the fields of Tyle House!

Our neighbour Sid Tucker from Old Muzzard, used to get water from the same well that we used. It was quite a walk, especially with two full buckets, but his wife needed water as she was churning butter. After filling the buckets, he stopped to pass the time of day with us at Kennexstone; George, in his bus, drove past so closely that he knocked over both the buckets. Sid had another long trek up the hill – and we could hear his wife calling out, "Sidney dear, where's the water?"

One Tuesday, my father and I went to Gowerton Mart on the bus, our cattle were being brought there in a lorry. The driver arrived without the cattle as he had been unable to reach Kennexstone because there had been a cloudburst, and the water was up over the bridge. When we returned home, we found that the stream outside the house had over-flowed and had come in through the front door and out of the back! Our piglets had been swimming around the yard and a young boy who helped us on the farm had climbed into a long zinc bath and managed to rescue them all!

A lamb that arrived late in the Spring was called a 'cuckoo lamb' as it was born after the arrival of the cuckoo.

A passer-by came to tell us one day that a young foal had been aban-doned nearby. We phoned around to try to find its owner, without success. As it was probably only a day old it needed to be fed, so we talked to a neighbour who knew about bottle-feeding foals, and she told us not to feed it with pure cow's milk, as mare's milk had a lot of lime in it. We bought some lime to mix with the milk and our Caravanners helped to feed it. It needed to be fed four times a day, and would come to the gate and call out when it was ready for another bottle. We called her Suzie, and she grew into a lovely little pony.

We also had a pet lamb that palled up with one of our kittens. We looked out one day and saw the kitten sleeping on the lamb's back whilst it was grazing. As the lamb grew older, it became a bit of a nuisance, so we put it out with the older sheep. About two months later, we brought the sheep down to the farm for shearing. The lamb came straight to the house, looking for the kitten, which jumped onto his back, and they went off happily together.

Caravanners feeding our pet lamb.

'The Cleveland' aground at Llangennith.

On the 28th June 1957, *The Cleveland*, a Hunt Class destroyer that was being towed to a breaker's yard broke free from its towrope and came aground near Diles Lake, Llangennith. All attempts by tugs to re-float her failed, and she was finally broken up on the beach. The destroyer proved to be a great tourist attraction.

I have always been involved in the community around me. Like my father before me, I am Secretary of Bethesda Chapel, Burry Green. Generations of my family have worshipped there, and I was carried there in my mother's arms as a baby. Many of my ancestors are buried in its graveyard.

I have also been Chairman of the Community Council, Chairman of the Gower Show, and of the Farmers' Union.

Gower Show, 1951.
(By kind permission of Robert Davies, Knelston).

Glyn and Ivy celebrating their Ruby Wedding with their grandchildren,
Victoria, Jessica, Mark and Marianne.

I have seen great changes in Gower – the days of farm workers coming
to our house for a game of bagatelle under the oil lamp have long gone,
but we enjoyed such simple pleasures. Tractors have replaced horses;
potato planters and precision drills have made the farmer's life much
easier. But there was a wonderful community spirit in those days when
we all had to help each other, and some wonderful characters around
who could always tell a good story!

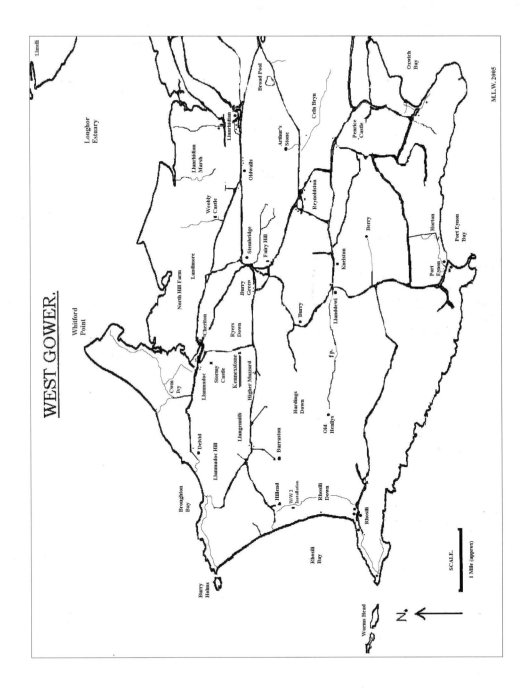

WEST GOWER.

Acknowledgements

For their assistance in compiling this book, Glyn Rogers and Llanrhidian History Group would like to thank –

Cynthia Austin
Gwyneth Bevan, Cwm Ivy
Richard Brighton at the Cambrian Index
Wilma Collins
Gwyn Davies, Swansea Reference Library
Michael Gibbs
Gower Church Magazines
Cathy & Eleanor Jenkins
Randolph Jenkins, M.Sc., B.Sc.
Eddie John, Dinefwr Press – for his professional assistance
Anne Karim, proofreader
Susan Medwell, B.A.
South Wales Evening Post
The County Archivist for access to the Llanmadoc School log-books. They are held at the West Glamorgan Archive Service.

And Martin, who, with the assistance of Alex & Harry Heather, has with great patience, enhanced all the photographs and farm accounts.

The co-ordinators of Llanrhidian History Group – Dave Elliott, Cindy Hyde, Anne Karim and Pat Williams – would also like to thank the North Gower Hotel, Llanrhidian, for the use of the hotel facilities for their meetings.